STUDY GUIDE FOR
INTERIOR FREEDOM

STUDY GUIDE FOR

INTERIOR

FREEDOM •• Jacques Philippe

Marie Thibodeau

 Scepter

Published by Scepter Publishers, Inc.
info@scepterpublishers.org
www.scepterpublishers.org
800-322-8773
New York

Text and cover design by Rose Design

ISBN: 978-1-59417-289-2 (pbk)
ISBN: 978-1-59417-290-8 (ebook)

First Printing

Printed in the United States of America.

CONTENTS

WEEK I

• • • •

Interior Freedom pages 9–31

Introduction

1. St. Paul tells us that, "Where the Spirit of the Lord is, there is freedom." (2 Corinthians 3:17) (page 9)

   What do you think St. Paul means by freedom?

   _____

   _____

   _____

   _____

   _____

2. Fr. Philippe states, "Every Christian needs to discover that even in the most unfavorable outward circumstances we possess within ourselves a space of freedom that nobody can take away, because God is its source and guarantee." (page 9)

   Have you ever known or read about someone whom you would identify as being truly free? Can

7

you describe them? What do you think was the
source of their freedom?

_____

_____

_____

_____

_____

Chapter I. Freedom and Acceptance

1. Fr. Philippe describes the modern era as being
   characterized by a search for freedom but states,
   ". . . false ideas of freedom have alienated
   people from the truth and caused millions of
   deaths." (page 12)

   Can you think of some examples of suffering that
   have been caused by false ideas of freedom?

   _____

   _____

   _____

_____

_____

2. "The kind of love that is the result of constraint, or self-interest, or the mere satisfaction of a need, does not deserve the name love." (page 13)

How would you describe true love and why is freedom an essential precondition to its development?

_____

_____

_____

_____

_____

3. "For modern man, to be free often means throwing off all constraint and all authority." (page 14)

How does this contrast with the Christian understanding of freedom?

_____

_____

_____

_____

_____

4. "As long as our sense of having greater or less
   freedom depends on outward circumstances, it
   means that we are not yet truly free."
   (footnote page 15)

   Do you ever lie awake at night, struggling with
   family stresses or problems in your job, for
   example? If these issues were resolved, you would
   finally be free to live the life you want? If the
   basis of your peace is a life free of struggle, do
   you think you can ever achieve that?

   _____

   _____

   _____

   _____

   _____

5. "It is in your own heart that you are restricted."
   (page 17)

How does our lack of love restrict our hearts
or conversely, how does loving God and others
more intensely make our hearts expand?

_____

_____

_____

_____

6. "They can't do anything to us, they really can't."
   Etty Hillesum (page 23)

   Since Etty, was in no way denying the power of
   the Nazis to inflict harm on her, what does she
   mean by this statement and how does it make
   you reflect on difficult circumstances or limitations in your own life?

   _____

   _____

   _____

   _____

   _____

7. "Love, and only love, can overcome evil by good and draw good out of evil." (page 25)

   Can you think of an example from your own life or the life of someone you know, where love overcame evil or was ultimately able to draw good from it?

   _____

   _____

   _____

   _____

   _____

8. "When we are faced with things that we find unpleasant or consider negative, in ourselves or in our situation, there are three possible attitudes." (page 29)

   What are these three approaches? Can you identify times when you dealt with reality by rebelling? Have you ever become resigned, allowing a sense of hopelessness to overtake you? How might things have been different if you had consented to these situations instead?

_____

_____

_____

_____

_____

9. Real freedom, Fr. Philippe says, "is consenting to what we did not originally choose." (page 28)

This week's challenge: Are there problems you find are difficult to bear? Try and apply this principle to those situations and see if doing so transforms your reality for the better.

PRAYER

Dear Lord, I want to experience this kind of freedom, a freedom not based on circumstances but rather on You. Help me to recognize those areas in my life which rob me of joy and please teach me to consciously embrace them with Your love.

WEEK II

• • • •

Interior Freedom pages 31—44

Before we begin this week's study, let us recap last week's challenge. We were asked to "consent to what we did not originally choose." Was anyone able to apply this teaching to a difficult circumstance or area of life and if so, what was the result?

1. "The great secret of all spiritual fruitfulness and growth is learning to let God act." (page 32)

   Are you surprised by this secret? Do you tend to believe that God expects you to work hard and become holier through your own strength?

   _____

   _____

   _____

   _____

   _____

2. "The person God loves with the tenderness of a Father, the person he wants to touch and to transform with his love, is not the person we'd have liked to be or ought to be." (page 32)

Close your eyes for a minute and imagine that you are sitting with God. How does he look at you? Is his expression one of love? Do you struggle to think of God loving you just as you are?

_____

_____

_____

_____

_____

3. "We must accept ourselves just as we are, if the Holy Spirit is to change us for the better." (page 33)

How does failing to accept our real selves impede the action of the Holy Spirit in our souls?

_____

_____

_____

_____

_____

4. "Someone might object that this idea of the need to 'consent to what we are,' with all our deficiencies and limitations, signifies mere passivity and laziness." (page 34)

How can we strive to answer God's call to become perfect and yet at the same time learn to totally and unconditionally accept ourselves as we truly are?

_____

_____

_____

_____

_____

5. "Accepting ourselves is much more difficult than it might seem." (page 35)

What stops most of us from facing the truth about ourselves? Why do we so often blame others, or make excuses rather than taking responsibility for our weaknesses and faults?

_____

_____

_____

_____

_____

6. Henri Nouwen admitted, "For a very long time I considered low self-esteem to be some kind of virtue." (page 37)

Have you ever believed that putting yourself down was an effective antidote to pride? Why is this a false remedy and how does it offend God?

_____

_____

_____

_____

_____

7. "The standards of success dictated by contemporary culture weigh on us much more heavily

than the appeal to perfectionism made by Jesus." (page 39)

The world urges us to be someone we are not, while at the same time God inspires us to strive for holiness; how can we discriminate between these two voices?

_____

_____

_____

_____

_____

8. "In consenting to what we are, we accept ourselves in our poverty but also in our richness . . ." (page 42)

What does this statement mean to you and how would you contrast it with our tendency to hang on to self-limiting beliefs?

_____

_____

_____

9. "Often, we fail to accept others because deep down, we do not accept ourselves." (page 43)

Why do you think that our difficulties with accepting others is interrelated with how we view ourselves?

_____

_____

_____

_____

_____

10. "Even if we fall every day, as long as we get up again and say, 'Lord, thank you, because I'm sure that you will make me a saint!' we give immense pleasure to God and sooner or later will receive from him what we hope for." (page 40)

This week's challenge: Decide to respond in this manner whenever you are confronted with your weaknesses and sinful tendencies. With each fall

19

make an act of faith in God's power to transform you into a saint!

PRAYER

Lord, when I consider my weaknesses and failings, the sins I have committed, and the sins that I am likely to commit in the future, I find it difficult to believe that I can ever become holy. Yet, I know that this is the desire of Your heart and that it is also the desire of my heart. Show me the way Lord. Help me, no matter how many times I may fall, to keep my eyes fixed on Your loving face!

WEEK III

• • • •

Interior Freedom pages 44–60

Last week, we were inspired to give God joy by exercising confidence in his love for us and in his desire to make us saints. Were you truly able to thank him immediately after a fall or in your weaknesses?

1. "We cannot change our lives effectively unless we begin by accepting them, welcoming them totally, and so consenting to all the external events that confront us." (page 44)

   Is learning to accept our life, with all its pain and limitations, merely a passive approach to dealing with our problems? Why or why not?

   _____

   _____

   _____

   _____

   _____

2. "Peaceful suffering is no longer suffering." (Curé of Ars, St. Jeanne Marie Vianney page 46)

   Have you ever experienced or witnessed *peaceful suffering*? What does this mean?

   _____

   _____

   _____

   _____

   _____

3. "What really hurts is not so much suffering itself as the fear of suffering." (page 47)

   How can the fear of suffering be harder to bear than the reality of it?

   _____

   _____

   _____

   _____

   _____

4. "To be able to enter little by little into God's wisdom, infinitely more beautiful, richer, more fruitful, and more merciful than ours, our human wisdom needs a very thorough shake-up." (page 51)

What does it mean to have your wisdom shaken up and what do you think would ultimately happen to you if your life always unfolded just as you planned or desired?

_____

_____

_____

_____

_____

5. "The motives behind our desire to understand may not always be upright." (page 52)

How does God use times of darkness and confusion to draw us into a deeper level of trust in him? Have you ever experienced this form of purification?

_____

_____

_____

_____

_____

6. "Even if we do all we can to find out God's will
   in this or that situation by prayer, reflection, and
   spiritual guidance, we will not always get a very
   clear answer, at least not right away." (page 54)

   What should you do if after availing yourself of
   all appropriate means, you still lack direction on
   how to proceed?

_____

_____

_____

_____

_____

7. "Our freedom always has this marvelous power
   to make what is taken from us—by life, events, or
   other people—into something offered." (page 57)

Give an example of this offering from what you
have read or from your own life experience. What
would you say can be the effect of such an offering?

_____

_____

_____

_____

_____

8. "The feeling of being helpless and powerless
   is a painful trial, especially when it concerns
   someone close to us: to see someone we love in
   difficulties without being able to help is one of
   the bitterest sufferings there is." (page 58–59)

   Do you agree that this is perhaps the most painful trial of all? What does Fr. Philippe encourage
   us to do when we are unable to prevent the
   suffering of our loved ones?

_____

_____

_____

_____

_____

9. "Love though bereft of means and apparently powerless, is always fruitful." (page 59)

This week's challenge: Think about a relationship or situation in which you feel helpless and ask God to show you how to love fruitfully.

PRAYER

Dear God, I ask you to show me how to love with your love, especially during those times in which I feel most helpless. My attempts to fix the problem or to take other equally unhealthy approaches are robbing me of peace. Help me to abandon my problems to Your love and to learn to join my sufferings to Yours so that one day they may bear great fruit.

WEEK IV

• • • •

Interior Freedom pages 60–80

At the end of last week's study, we were not only challenged to identify when we feel most helpless but to invoke God's assistance in learning how to love fruitfully in our suffering. Can you share how this affected your approach to difficulties? Did you experience a new awareness of God's presence or help?

1. "Hard as it is, we need to learn to forgive other people for making us suffer or disappointing us, and even to accept the problems they create for us as graces and blessings." (page 61)

   When Fr. Philippe encourages us to accept sufferings that are caused by the free will of others, is he saying that we should not address wrongs or stand up for ourselves in certain situations?

   _____

   _____

   _____

_____

_____

2. "People have very different and sometimes
   conflicting temperaments and ways of seeing
   things, and that is something to be recognized
   and accepted cheerfully." (page 61)

   Why is it important to accept the differences in
   other people's personalities that do not always
   jive well with our own disposition? How can
   accepting people in this way, help us to mature
   and live a fuller and more contented life?

   _____

   _____

   _____

   _____

   _____

3. "The only way to diminish the suffering that
   burdens mankind is by forgiveness." (page 63)

   Do you believe that an attitude of forgiveness can
   diminish suffering in your life and the lives of

those you love? Can you think of a time in your life, when you forgave someone or when someone extended unconditional forgiveness to you? Was this a moment of healing for you?

_____

_____

_____

_____

_____

4. "It bears repeating, however, that unless we understand the importance of forgiveness and practice it in our relations with others, we will never achieve inner freedom but will always be prisoners of our own bitterness." (page 64)

We have all tasted the bitterness that festers when we find ourselves unable or unwilling to forgive. What kind of power does unforgiveness exercise over a person and what is its effect on the psyche?

_____

_____

_____

_____

_____

5. "Sometimes we think, consciously or sub-
consciously, that forgiving someone who has
wronged us would mean pretending they had
done nothing wrong—calling bad good, or
condoning an act of injustice." (page 64)

Would you agree with this observation? Do you
think that in addition to this, we may also struggle with a desire to see that person pay for the
wrong they have done us? Is it difficult to leave
judgement to God?

_____

_____

_____

_____

_____

6. Chapter 6, verse 38 of St. Luke's gospel states,
"For the measure you give will be the measure
you get back." (page 67)

Often this text is cited as a warning of what will happen to us when we do not forgive our enemies but Fr. Philippe teaches us that within these words, the Lord is making us a wonderful promise. What is this promise and have you ever looked at this verse in this light? Does it encourage you?

_____

_____

_____

_____

_____

7. "The devil often tries to discourage us and make us lose our joy in serving God." (page 73)

Have you sometimes fallen prey to these stratagems when you are attempting to accomplish some good? How should we combat this type of attack?

_____

_____

_____

_____

_____

8. "With apologies to those I am going to scandalize, I say that the evil around us—the sins of others, of people in the Church, of society—does not become an evil for us unless we let it penetrate our hearts." (page 75)

Are most people used to looking at evil or suffering in this manner? Do you find this statement challenging? If someone does evil to us, of course we experience suffering, so what exactly does Fr. Philippe mean when he says this?

_____

_____

_____

_____

_____

9. "St. Maximilian Kolbe died in a starvation bunker at Auschwitz, but his heart remained pure and intact in that hellish place, because he felt

no hatred for his executioners and consented to give up his life for love." (page 78)

How can we learn to live and die like this great man? What will help us react to evil in a manner that does not cause us harm but instead liberates us and transforms us into saints?

---

10. "We are kings because we are children and heirs of the King of heaven and earth. But also in the sense that we are subjects to nothing and everything is subject to us." (page 79)

This week's challenge: Reflect on the character you received at baptism, when you were anointed as God's very own child. Ask God to show you how your adoption into his family enables you to be subject to nothing of this earth.

PRAYER

Lord, I believe your word. I know that when I do not forgive, I poison my own soul and deprive myself of your grace. Show me any vestiges of unforgiveness that I may be harboring. I want to live a life of freedom, claiming my heritage as your beloved child.

WEEK V

Interior Freedom pages 81–93

Chapter 2. The Present Moment

At the end of last week's meeting we were challenged to spend time reflecting on our identity as God's cherished children. Was this a shift in the way you normally regard yourself? How did this perspective impact the manner in which you faced your daily struggles over this past week?

1. "The only free act we can make in regard to the past is to accept it just as it was and leave it trustingly in God's hands." (page 81)

   Sometimes we fear quiet moments because suddenly out of nowhere a memory of a past sin or mistake will appear to torment us and make us feel regret for what we have done or lost. How do you typically handle these kinds of thoughts when they arise? According to Fr. Philippe, what should you do?

   _____

   _____

_____

_____

_____

2. "God is the eternal present." (page 82)

   If God is accessible to us only in the present
   moment, how should this change the way
   we approach our past and our future? What
   about our present? Think of times during
   your day when you are beset by struggles; what
   might happen if instead of getting angry or
   frustrated you chose to remember that God is
   with you, in fact, closer to you than you are to
   yourself?

_____

_____

_____

_____

_____

3. "I often say jokingly that the ladder of perfection
   has only one step: the step we take today." (page 83)

Does this seem too simple to you? Why or why not?

_____

_____

_____

_____

_____

4. "Projecting things into the future crushes us—
   not experiencing suffering but anticipating it."
   (page 85)

   Have you ever been tormented by a fear of things
   that never ended up happening? By contrast,
   when trials came that you never imagined, did you
   suddenly discover unexpected strength and the
   grace to endure them? If so, when was it given?

_____

_____

_____

_____

5. "We often complain about how much we are suffering, without realizing that it's our fault." (page 85)

   Would most people be shocked or perhaps offended by this assertion? What exactly does Fr. Philippe mean when he says that sometimes we are the cause of our own suffering? Have you ever made your suffering worse by your negative attitude? What could you have done differently?

   _____

   _____

   _____

   _____

   _____

6. "If it's a mistake to add the burden of the past to the weight of the present, it's a still worse mistake to burden the present with the future." (page 87)

   What happens to us when we are unable to fully live in the present? Have you experienced negative physical or emotional effects from either regret or worry? Was there a turning point in which you ultimately discovered relief or healing?

_____

_____

_____

_____

_____

7. "At present we tell ourselves, we don't really have a life, but later we will 'live life to the full.'" (page 90)

Can excessive day dreaming or misplaced hope in our future take a toll on how we face our present reality? Do you struggle with the conviction that your 'real' life will finally begin once certain things change?

_____

_____

_____

_____

8. "It doesn't matter whether the job we have in hand is sweeping the kitchen floor or giving speech to forty-thousand people. We must put our hearts into it, simply and calmly, and not try to solve more than one problem at a time." (page 91)

Think about your routines and the tasks you must accomplish on a regular basis: grocery shopping, cleaning the kitchen, cooking etc. Are there some you do mindlessly, even begrudgingly, just pushing through until you can finally deal with what *really* matters? Could giving your full attention to one task at a time relieve stress or increase contentment?

_____

_____

_____

_____

_____

9. "A heart preoccupied by concerns and worries isn't available to other people." (page 91)

Have you ever tried talking with someone who is preoccupied? How did you feel?

_____

_____

_____

_____

_____

10. "In every encounter with someone else, however long or short, we should make him feel we're one hundred percent there for him at that moment, with nothing else to do except be with him and do whatever needs doing for him." (page 91)

Do you think that Fr. Philippe means that in order to be completely present to someone, you might need to let the dinner burn or the baby scream, for example? How is it possible to be completely available to someone with so many often-conflicting demands on your time?

_____

_____

_____

_____

_____

11. "It might be said that there are two modes of time: time of the head and time of the heart." (page 92)

We are all familiar with psychological time, or the time of the head but have you ever experienced what Fr. Philippe refers to as the time of the heart? How did the saints learn to live by this interior time? What did it cost them?

_____

_____

_____

_____

_____

This week's challenge: Begin learning to live according to the time of the heart by abandoning yourself to God's plans in regard to your concerns. When people or duties pull at you simultaneously, invoke the Holy Spirit and his

wisdom so that all may be accomplished lovingly and calmly.

PRAYER

Lord, it is so difficult to let go of my agenda. I am easily frustrated and anxious whenever someone or something disrupts or derails my plans. Please help me to focus on seeking your will in the present moment and teach me to trust completely in you rather than my own efforts.

WEEK VI

· · · ·

Interior Freedom pages 94–110

Chapter 3. The Dynamism of Faith, Hope, and Love

1. "The theological virtues have a key role in the spiritual life because here our freedom and God's grace cooperate." (page 95)

   Why are the virtues of faith, hope and love central to our growth in maturity and how do they work with our free will? Can you think of times when despite long suffering, you have continued to trust in God's faithfulness? Have you sometimes made, for example, a conscious decision to love an enemy?

   _____

   _____

   _____

   _____

   _____

2. "Just as the Rosary contains joyful, sorrowful and finally glorious mysteries, it could be said of the work of the Holy Spirit in our lives that there are 'outpourings' that are joyful, sorrowful, and glorious." (pages 97–98)

What is the purpose of each of these three distinct outpourings of the Spirit in our life?

_____

_____

_____

_____

_____

3. "The first outpouring of the Holy Spirit in St. Peter's life occurred at the moment of his vocation, when he felt impelled to leave everything—job, nets, boat, and family—to follow Jesus." (page 98)

Have you ever heard God calling you to take an unexpected path? Were there things that you left behind to follow his voice? How did this moment become a joyful outpouring of the Spirit in your life?

_____

_____

_____

_____

_____

4. "And Peter broke down in tears, in which his
   heart was purified there and then." (page 100)

   In what way, did Peter's denial of Christ occasion
   a sorrowful outpouring of the Spirit? How was
   Peter's response different than that of Judas?
   What holds *you* back from running straight into
   the arms of Jesus as soon as your conscience
   convicts you of sin?

_____

_____

_____

_____

_____

5. "Burning with the charity poured out in his heart by the Holy Spirit, Peter from then on was a tireless Apostle, rejoicing in his opportunities to suffer for the name of Jesus." (page 101)

The outpouring of the Holy Spirit on those in the upper room, was certainly dramatic and powerful, yet all of us today are called to receive this glorious outpouring of the Spirit as well. Have you been Confirmed? If so how do you think this experience affected your life? Is Confirmation the only time in which a follower of Christ might receive this type of glorious outpouring?

_____

_____

_____

_____

_____

6. "We should abandon ourselves trustingly to God, sure that sooner or later [our] wretchedness will be transformed into burning charity." (page 102)

It's one thing to sit beside a cozy fire and quite another to become engulfed in its flames yet,

St. John teaches us that in order to become holy, our souls must be moved from the arm chair into the blaze. Does it frighten you to think that your wretchedness must be exposed and purified by a trial of fire? Why should we welcome such a process?

_____

_____

_____

_____

_____

7. "When we lose fervor, zest, generosity in loving God and neighbor, it is very often because of discouragement or even a sort of secret despair." (page 105)

   Think of people you may know who have become bitter or hardened; in what or whom were they trusting? Contrast them with Jeremiah's admonition, "Blessed is the man who trusts in the Lord, whose trust is the Lord." (Jeremiah 17:7)

_____

_____

_____

_____

_____

8. "Lack of trust in what God's grace can do in our
   lives, and what we can do with his help, leads to
   a shrinkage of the heart, a lessening of charity."
   (page 105)

   What happens to love in relationships that are not
   based on trust? Can our love for God grow cold if
   we are not consciously relying on his help?

_____

_____

_____

_____

_____

9. "God does not give according to our merits, but
   according to our hope." (page 107)

Do you sometimes hope in things that are illusory or not worthy of your desire? Will God allow you to be satisfied with anything less than himself?

_____

_____

_____

_____

_____

10. "Faith is the root of our cure and our liberation, the start of a life-giving process that heals the death engendered by sin." (page108)

    The fall of our first parents began with a lack of faith in God which eventually led to sin. Have you noticed a similar pattern in your life? What kinds of things or situations most acutely affect your trust in God? What should you do whenever you recognize that you are not trusting in God?

    _____

    _____

    _____

_____

_____

11. "Impurity of heart is duplicity the prophets denounced so often: that of people who, lacking complete trust in God, pray to idols, shopping around for salvation." (page 110)

We don't often picture people today worshipping idols and yet, if we put our trust in anyone or anything besides God, we are in a sense worshipping false idols. What are some of the false idols in our culture? Are there little idols in your life that you run to first for help, before you finally turn to God? Why do you think that Deuteronomy chapter 4 verse 24 states: "For the Lord your God is a devouring fire, a jealous God."

_____

_____

_____

_____

_____

This week's challenge: Reflect on how you can grow in virtue. Think of the different outpourings of the Holy Spirit and ask him to highlight at least one situation in which you can, with the assistance of God's grace, choose to believe, to hope or to love.

PRAYER

Lord, I admit that when I am struggling or in pain, I don't always run to you first. Often, in fact, I look elsewhere for comfort or assistance or I foolhardily attempt to solve things myself. Please help me to rely on you alone and cleanse my soul of idols with the fire of your mercy.

WEEK VII

• • • •

Interior Freedom pages 111–134

Chapter 4. From Law to Grace: Love as a Free Gift

1. "For freedom Christ has set us free; stand fast therefore, and do not submit again to a yoke of slavery." (Galatians 5:1) (page III)

   In your opinion, does the average person in the pew believe that Christ died to set them free from the yoke of slavery? What exactly is a yoke and what does it mean to be yoked to sin? By contrast, how would you describe a life of freedom in Christ?

   _____

   _____

   _____

   _____

   _____

2. "What the law tells us to do is good. But taking the law as the foundation for our relationship to God contradicts the truth that salvation is given freely and ends up killing love." (page 115)

How is it possible that the law, which God inspired, can become a trap for some people and how does it lead to pride and ultimately despair?

_____

_____

_____

_____

_____

3. "It doesn't come naturally to us to *give freely.*" (page 117)

What is often at the root of the "love" we extend towards others? How do you feel when someone gives you something but you know that it is not given freely?

_____

_____

_____

_____

_____

4. "We are happy to receive something seen as in
   some way a reward for our merits, something due
   us." (page 118)

   What kind of person is able to receive something
   that they did not merit? Why does Fr. Philippe
   say that unless we learn to give and to receive
   freely, we shall never be happy?

_____

_____

_____

_____

_____

Chapter 5. Spiritual Poverty and Freedom

1. "We need to know who we are; we need to exist
   in our own eyes and other people's" (page 120)

Our need for identity can lead us to try and find it in all the wrong places. What are some ways that people attempt to define themselves outside of God? What is the ultimate result of doing this?

_____

_____

_____

_____

_____

2. "When the Gospel says we must 'die to ourselves,' it means this artificial ego, this constructed self, must die, so that the real 'self' given us by God can emerge." (page 122)

What is an artificial ego and why do we construct it? Why is this an especially dangerous tendency in the spiritual life?

_____

_____

_____

_____

3. "This is why humility, spiritual poverty, is so precious: it locates our identity securely in the one place where it will be safe from all harm." (page 124)

   How does this relate to Jesus' admonition from the Gospel of Matthew: "Everyone then who hears these words of mine and does them will be like a wise man who built his house upon the rock; and the rain fell, and the floods came, and the winds blew and beat upon that house, but it did not fall because it was founded on the rock"? (Matthew 7:24–25)

   _____

   _____

   _____

   _____

   _____

4. "The trials of 'purification' so frequently referred to by the mystics are there to destroy whatever is artificial in our character, so that

our true being may emerge—i.e., what we are to God." (page 125–126)

What eventually becomes apparent to the soul who clings to God despite being stripped of fervor or any sensible feelings towards him? Do you tend to measure your relationship with God by how you feel? Have you experienced a period of extended dryness and wondered if God was displeased with you?

---

5. "'Mature' Christians, who have truly become children of God, are those who have experienced their radical nothingness, their absolute poverty, been reduced to nothing." (page 129)

If a person has been reduced to nothing by trials of purification, how is it that they abound in joy and freedom? Why are they no longer downcast at the sight of their weaknesses and what makes them so attractive to others?

_____

_____

_____

_____

_____

6. "The people who are supremely free desire nothing and are afraid of nothing. All the good that
   matters to them is already guaranteed them by
   God." (page 130)

   For you to become truly free, God will use all
   your trials, disappointments, failures and even
   your sins to liberate you from your false self. How
   can you then cooperate in a manner that makes
   his work in your soul more efficacious and if
   possible, less painful?

_____

_____

_____

_____

_____

Has this study drawn you closer to God and opened your eyes to the nature of true freedom? How will you challenge yourself to go forward now that this study is completed?

_____

_____

_____

_____

_____

FINAL PRAYER

Jesus, I desire true freedom from the slavery of sin. I want above all to be united to you. Teach me to see your loving design at work in my sins, weaknesses and sufferings. Take my past and transform my regrets into bountiful blessings. Help me to live in the ever present now where all things are possible and to surrender my future to your loving providence.

CATHOLIC BOOK
STUDY GUIDE

• • • •

When people gather for the purpose of prayerfully studying a book it is a very good idea to review certain guidelines before beginning. These guidelines may seem basic and self-evident, but reminding everyone of expectations can alleviate many potential glitches.

1. It is important to allow *all* members of the study to answer questions if they so chose. Talkative personalities can easily forget that a quieter person will not offer their opinions if there is not space within the conversation for them to speak. Being mindful of not dominating the conversation and of taking turns to answer the questions can result in a richer and more positive experience for everyone involved.

2. A book study that deals with spiritual struggles and growth can affect people deeply and may elicit very personal insights. However, it is essential to remember that the central purpose of the group is to reflect on the book and to share ideas that pertain to it. It is not the appropriate venue for sharing complicated personal problems or for advising participants on how to resolve family issues, etc.

3. Creating a welcoming and nonjudgmental atmosphere is essential and will foster productive discussion and spiritual growth. Participants may vary greatly in their understanding of the faith; nevertheless, they should be encouraged to express their opinion without fear of others reacting negatively.

4. It can be very easy for any group to go off on tangents, which is why the moderator should be mindful to gently guide the group back to the topic when the need arises. Following the prepared questions is a simple way to keep everyone on track and to direct the flow of conversation.

5. The studies provided should take approximately 1½ hours. It is better to try and begin and end the formal portion of the meeting at the designated times, and to save fellowship until you've completed the study.

6. Finally, always begin and end with prayer. Invoke, especially, the presence of the Holy Spirit. Ask him to guide and illuminate your minds and knit your hearts together in love. At the end, thank God for the gift of his presence and ask him to pour out his graces on all of you as you strive to apply to your life what you have learned together in your study.